Charles Randall's Designer Sketchfile

Draperies, Valances, Fabric Shades & Bedding

100s of Black & White Illustrations • 100s of Glorious Decorating Ideas

Charles Randall's Designer Sketchfile

Draperies, Valances, Fabric Shades & Bedding

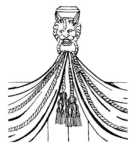

For my mother Peggy Randall
My "adopted mother" Dr. Carole Williams-Gelker Phd.
Esperanza Lucatero—my Hope and my Love
The Kimbrells
Your love during the completion of this book will never be forgotten.
—Charles Randall

Published in the United States by
Charles Randall Inc.
Orange, California

Distributed in Great Britain by
Antique Collectors Club Ltd
Woodbridge, Suffolk

Text and illustrations: Copyright 2006 Charles T. Randall
ISBN 1-890379-14-X
First United States Edition

Internet: www.randallonline.com
Illustrated by Burgundy Beam & Carlotta Tormey
Cover design by Diego Linares
Interior page design by Chemistry Creative, Minneapolis, MN
Edited by Kathleen S. Stoehr

Library of Congress Cataloging-in-Publication Data
Randall, Charles T.
  Charles Randall's designer sketchfile / by Charles Randall.
    p. cm.
  ISBN 1-890379-14-X
  1. Draperies in interior decoration. 2. Window shades. I. Title. II. Title: Designer sketchfile.
  NK2115.5.D73R35 2006
  747'.3--dc22
                        2006014386

Contents

Preface

I have compiled this sketchfile after many years of thought, as well as requests from designers, to offer a book of simple line art without the distraction of color. This book is about stretching your imagination, and pushing your creative talents. Remember that the design possibilities are endless if you embellish, add, remove or combine elements from other images. An example would be using a standard swag with gathered cascades—not necessarily shown in the book, but what you might take from one design and add to another. My hope in providing the CD ROM is that you, the designer, either professional or enthusiast, will break apart and then recompile elements to create totally custom, one-of-a-kind treatments. It's really exciting to have a custom design that is yours alone! If you add other elements to the design i.e., jabots, rosettes and trim—*voila!*—you have a unique design that reflects your individuality.

None of these designs will be found in my best-selling book: *The Encyclopedia of Windows Fashions.* Of course if you have a copy of *The Encyclopedia* or *Dream Windows* (another Charles Randall Inc. publication), all the better!

You will be amazed at what you can create and will hopefully take pride in creating something unique. After 20 years I must add that it's been quite a journey and I am so grateful to have traveled with many of you on this creative trip together.

Charles Randall

Draperies

Draperies

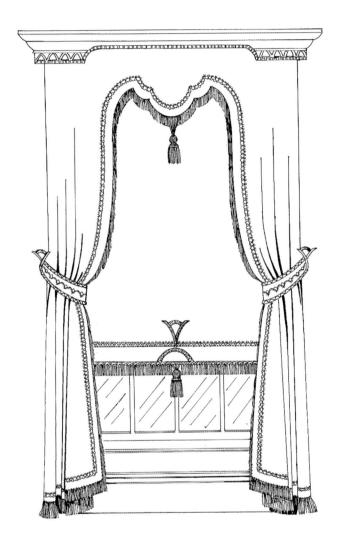

Image 101
A wood cornice tops this lovely stationary drapery treatment, accented with fringe and tassels and held back with decorative fabric tiebacks. A fringe trimmed shade provides privacy and sun control.

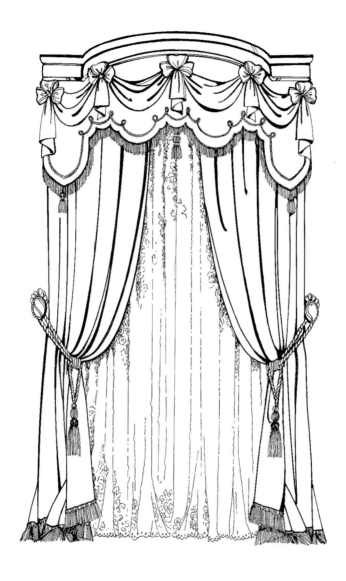

Image 102

An arched wood cornice caps a soft top treatment with fringe, accent cording and
jabots accented with bows, showcasing sheer lace underdraperies flanked with
bullion fringe-trimmed side panels, held back with tassel ties.

Draperies

Image 103

Elaborately styled swags hang gracefully from a soft cornice, ending in lushly
fringed cascades. Underneath, draperies contained by braid fringe and trimmed
tiebacks complete the window treatment.

Image 104

Double swags with petite bow accents cap a set of double drapery panels—one patterned, one plain. Lovely tassel tiebacks hold the fabric away from the window until night falls.

Draperies

Image 105

A wood cornice with sconce-like embellishments hold scalloped swags, trimmed
in fringe and accented with brush fringe, in style. Matching drapery panels
underneath are held back with braided tassels.

Image 106

A detailed wood cornice houses a fringed, cascade swag and top treatment, accented with tassel embellishments. Braid follows the leading edge of the sumptuous drapery panels with bullion fringe brushing the floor.

Draperies

Image 107

Goblet pleated drapery panels edged with pompom trim are accented with a swag and cascade top treatment and matching tiebacks.

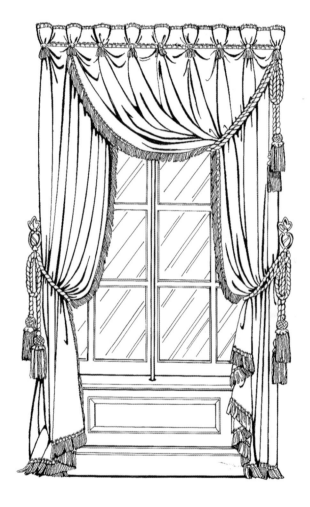

Image 108

This asymmetrical treatment is a stunning beauty with goblet pleats and bullion fringe. Note that the right hand panel has top and middle tassel tiebacks, which balance and enhance its beauty.

Draperies

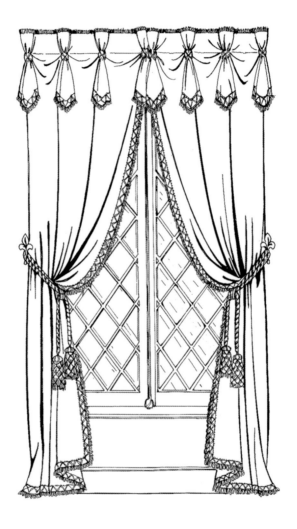

Image 109
Fringe-edged goblet pleated drapery panels with jabot accents are contained by
fleur de lys holdbacks and tassel ties.

Charles Randall's Designer Sketchfile

Image 110

A beautifully detailed wood cornice houses three treatments: a sheer undertreatment
to filter the light, a heavier overtreatment to mask the window entirely at night and
fringe-edged accent panels held in place with dramatic rosettes.

Draperies

Image 111
An asymmetrical pole swag, accented with a small rod pocket top treatment,
puddles on to the floor.

Charles Randall's Designer Sketchfile

Image 112
Unique string top drapery panels are held back with coordinating fabric tiebacks.

Draperies

Image 113
An empire valance accented with rosettes enhance simply pleated
drapery panels, held back with coordinating tiebacks.

Image 114
A strikingly trimmed empire valance complements the crisp pleats of the
stationary drapery panels.

Draperies

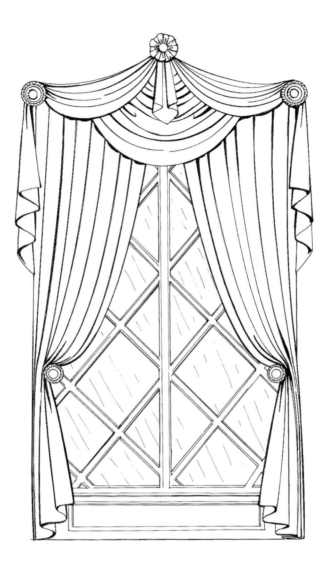

Image 115

Enhanced architectural interest is created by drawing elaborate swags up and
accenting with jabot and rosette. Cascades drape over crystal holdbacks on either
side of the window. Crystal holdbacks also contain the simple drapery panels.

Image 116
A lovely swag and cascade accented with petite tassel and trim, as well as rosettes.
Uncomplicated drapery panels serve as a backdrop.

Draperies

Image 117
Trim on the scalloped fabric shade is echoed in the soft swag and cascade cornice.
Note, too, that this is a four part treatment—both sheer and regular drapery
panels are employed.

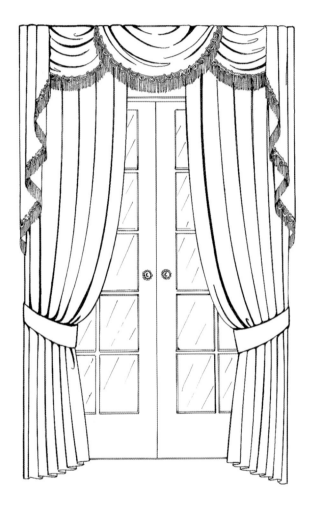

Image 118
A classic swag and cascade is trimmed in fringe and serves to hide the mechanisms
upon which the drapery panels are held in place.

Draperies

Image 119
Elaborately pleated cascades tumble down the sides of the stationary drapery
panels, enhanced by the three part swag above.

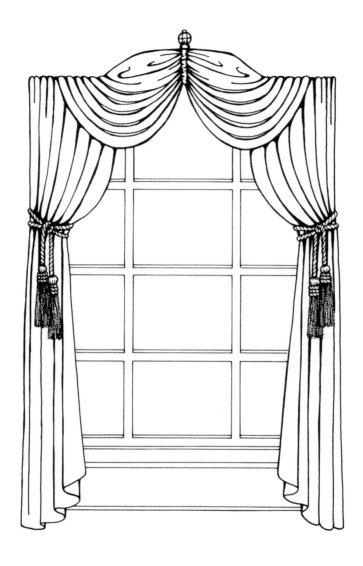

Image 120
Large tassels dangling from braided tiebacks create visual interest in this simple
but stunning treatment.

Draperies

Image 121

This asymmetrical swag and double cascade treatment with side panel accent is a perfect solution for sliding glass doors. Note how the bulk of the treatment resides in the non-egress area of the door.

Charles Randall's Designer Sketchfile

Image 122
A soft swag and jabot cornice eases gently over stationary, puddled side panels
edged in coordinating fabric.

Draperies

Image 123

A sheer undertreatment, puddled drapery panels, and a swag and cascade top treatment dripping with bullion fringe and braid are a regal combination.

Image 124
An asymmetrical pole swag edged in bullion fringe and accented with braided
tassel is classically beautiful.

Image 125

This crisp treatment includes swag and pleated cascade, stationary drapery panel,
all edged in petite tassel trim, and a fabric-covered three-inch pole.

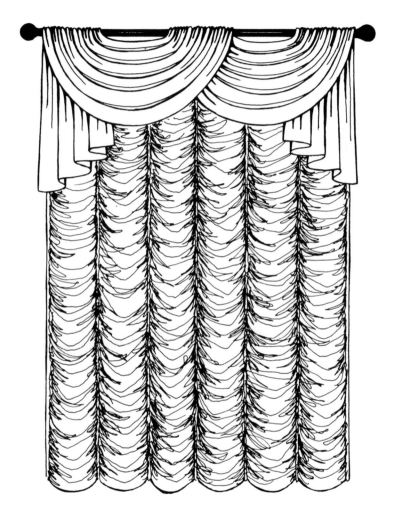

Image 126
An Austrian shade looks lovely under pole swags and cascades.

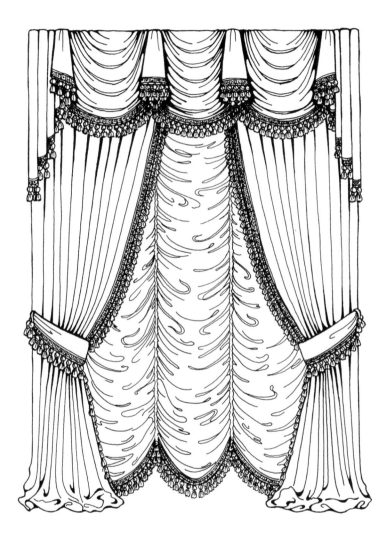

Image 127
This thoroughly elaborate treatment has been trimmed royally in thick passementerie: a Kingston valance, drapery panels, tiebacks and Italian strung underdraperies.

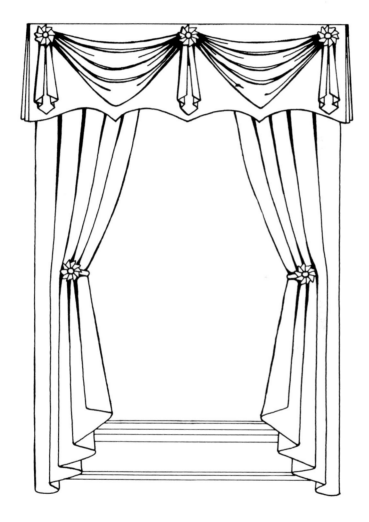

Image 128
A soft cornice is decorated with simple triangular swags and jabots, covering the tops of the drapery panels. Note how the rosettes are echoed, too, in the metal drapery holdbacks.

Draperies

Image 129
Swags and cascades are enhanced with thick bullion fringe and double braid
ropes. A sheet undertreatment and drapery panels are held back with tassels
and more braiding.

Image 130
A swag and cascade top treatment stylishly tops crisply pleated drapery panels with matching fabric tiebacks.

Draperies

Image 131
Sheer underdraperies are flanked with bullion trimmed side panels and a swag and
jabot top treatment with decorative trimmings.

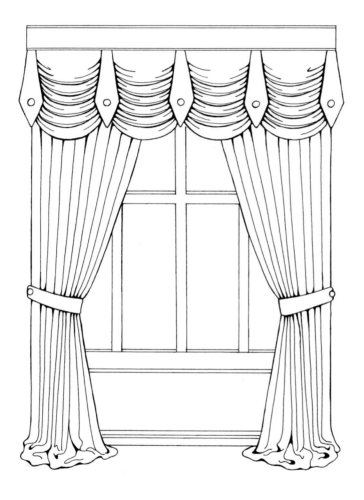

Image 132
An empire valance with jabots hangs from a plain wood cornice. Drapery panels
with matching fabric tiebacks puddle onto the floor.

Draperies

Image 133
A simple but elegant top treatment perfect for French doors: A pole swag with
lovely detailing draws attention but does not impede egress.

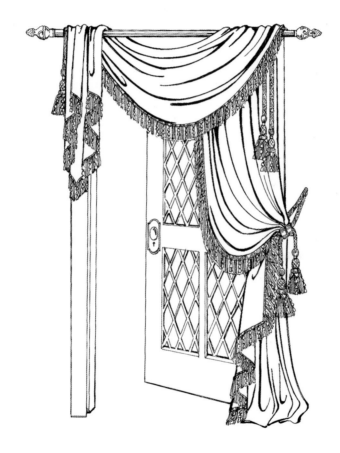

Image 134
An asymmetrical swag treatment is lushly detailed with bullion, tassels and plenty of thick, drapeable fabric.

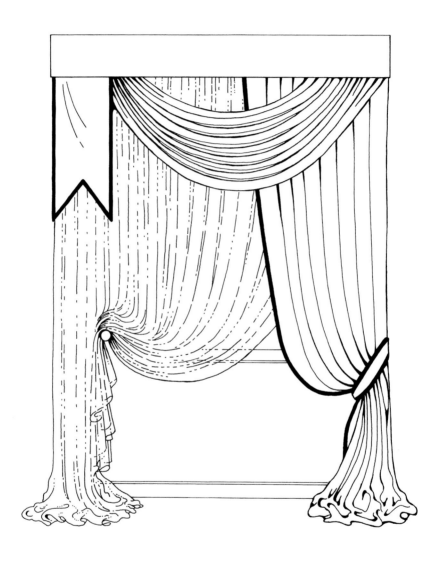

Image 135

To mask an unsightly view, a sheer underdrapery diffuses light, while the swag
and tail and right side drapery panel draw draw the eye away from the view.

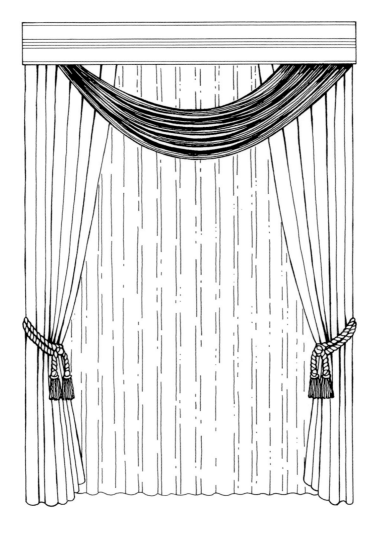

Image 136

A simple wood cornice houses all the hardware needed for hanging the sheer
underdrapery, side panels and single swag.

Draperies

Image 137
This unique treatment turns a rod pocket treatment on its side and then is installed
on the outside of an upholstered cornice, finishing in a double cascade. Stationary
drapery panels on either side are color blocked to pull the eye.

Image 138

Elaborate and lovely, fabric hangs in shabby chic swag and cascade style, layered over lush, puddled stationary drapery panels. Note how the braid lines the edge of the panels and then is also draped casually amongst the folds of the swag.

Draperies

Image 139

A two-layered treatment incorporates a sheer side panel, held back with tassel tieback and asymmetrical pole swag with bullion fringe and tassel tieback. The panel is easily released from its tieback to offer additional sun filtering.

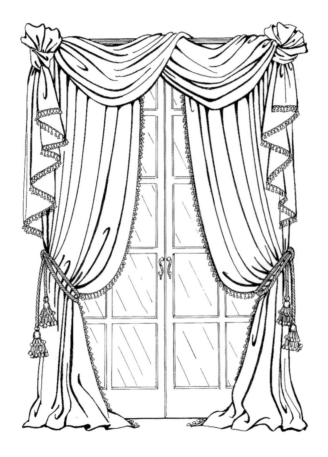

Image 140

A pole swag exhibits large decorative knots, which heightens the treatment visually and draws the eye. Side panels, held back with braided tassel trim, complete this stately, yet casual, look.

Draperies

Image 141
Sheer drapery treatments soften the view without masking it entirely.
An asymmetrical pole swag tops this treatment in style.

Image 142
Pencil pleated draperies are enhanced with intricate trim are held back from the
window invisibly to reveal a sheer undertreatment.

Draperies

Image 143
A legacy valance with goblet pleats and drapery panels offer a lush,
cozy feeling.

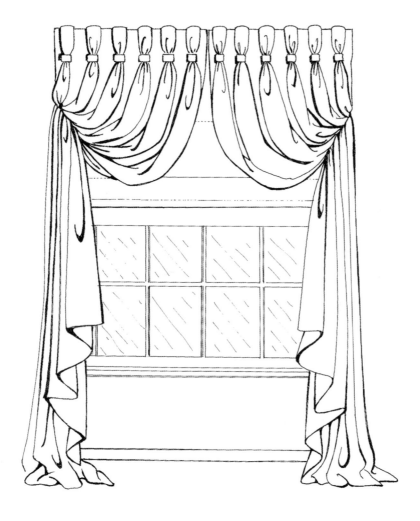

Image 144
Goblet pleated drapery panels cascade to the floor in easy elegance. A flat panel
Roman shade underneath provides the privacy and sun control.

Draperies

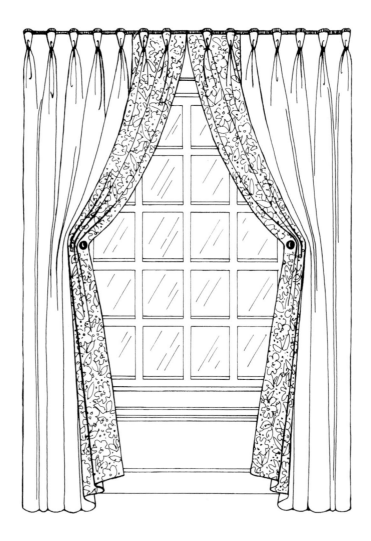

Image 145

A small window is made to look larger by placing the drapery panels higher and wider than the window itself. Note that the metal holdbacks for the dual-fabric panels must be placed on either side of the window frame for stability.

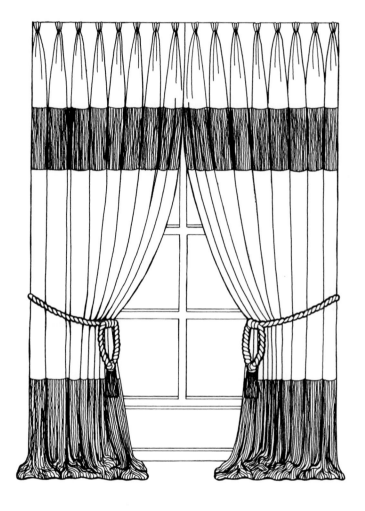

Image 146
Butterfly pleat drapery panels in a color block pattern are dramatic when
puddled onto the floor.

Draperies

Image 147

A deep goblet pleated top treatment works perfectly in this bay window with flanking, stationary drapery panels.

Image 148
Goblet pleated draperies with jabot accent are held back invisibly. Note the pretty braid and fringe trim.

Draperies

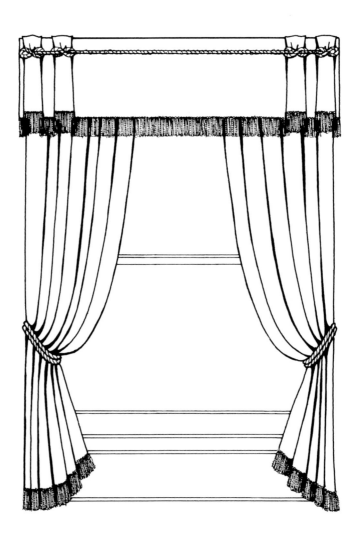

Image 149
A soft cartridge pleated cornice trimmed in brush fringe and braid tops pleated
drapery panels.

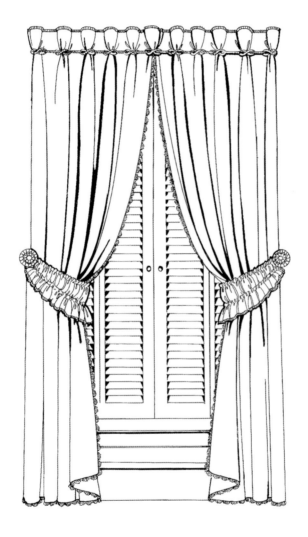

Image 150
Goblet pleated drapery panels with ornate fabric tiebacks soften hard shutter panels stylishly.

Draperies

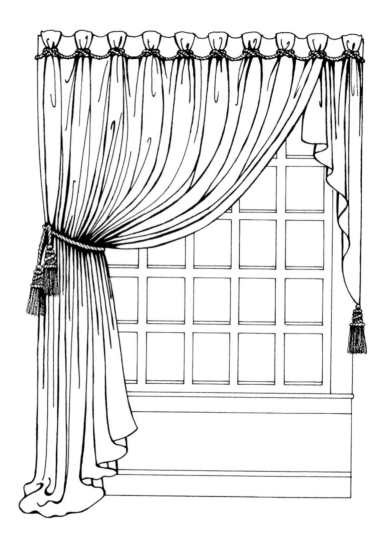

Image 151

An asymmetrical goblet pleated drapery treatment is enhanced with a tiny cascade
on the right hand side. Tassels and braiding make a fine detail.

Image 152

A rod pocket valance with cascades top simply pleated, traversing drapery
panels. Brush fringe is a terrific, eye-catching accent.

Draperies

Image 153
A scalloped flat rod pocket valance enhances the shape of the bay window and
hides the hanging hardware for the stationary drapery panels.

Deep box pleats create a dramatic top treatment, accenting lush drapery panels,
edged with cording.

Draperies

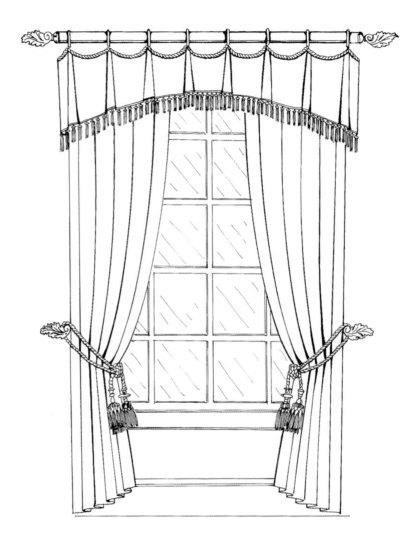

Image 155

A scalloped ring top valance with inverted box pleats, edged in tiny tassel fringe,
complements the pleated drapery panels—which can easily be released from their
holdbacks to provide privacy at night.

Uniquely gathered ring top drapery panels are doubled up to draw the eye to the center of the treatment, showcasing the intricate fringe and bead trim.

Draperies

Image 157
Legacy valances, hung with rings, enhance the slouchy, casual drapery panels.

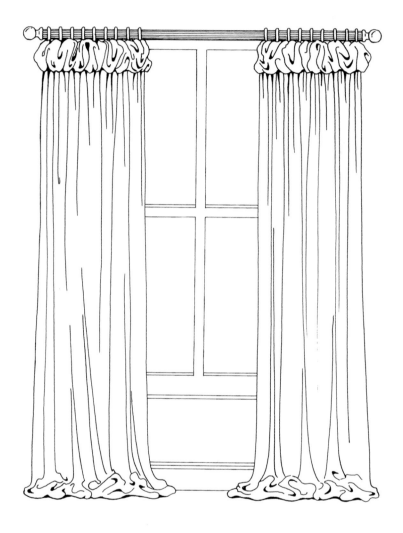

Image 158
Puddled blouson drapery panels, hung with rings, offer casual elegance.

Draperies

Image 159
A highly detailed wood cornice holds elegantly trimmed drapery panels, beautifully
simple and elegant.

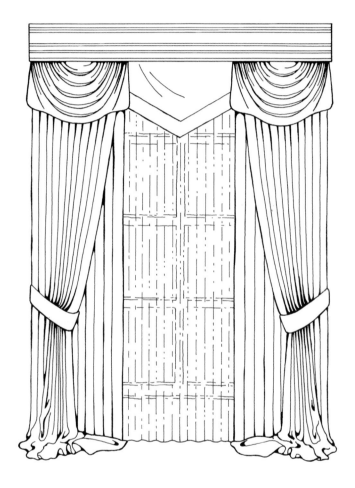

Image 160

The wood cornice not only provides architectural interest but also conceals the
five part treatment underneath it: sheer underdraperies, traversing overdraperies,
stationary side panels, flanking swags and a triangle valance.

Draperies

Image 161

This beautiful wood cornice draws the eye; the stationary side panels provide softness and color to any room decor.

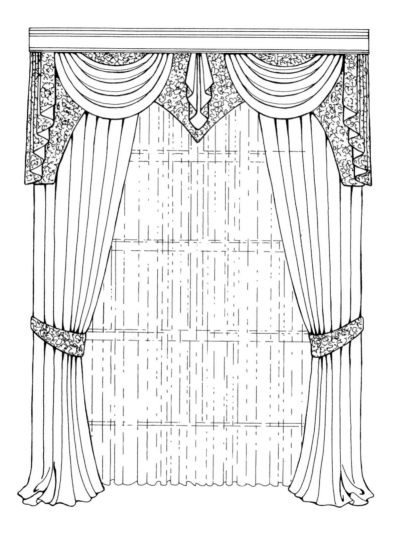

Image 162

An unsightly view is diffused through the employment of sheer draperies. To draw additional focus away from the out-of-doors, an elaborate swag, jabot and cascade treatment, soft cornice and drapery panels are a beautiful distraction.

Draperies

Image 163
Grommet topped panels make a simple, clean statement; fabric provides hopped
up visual interest.

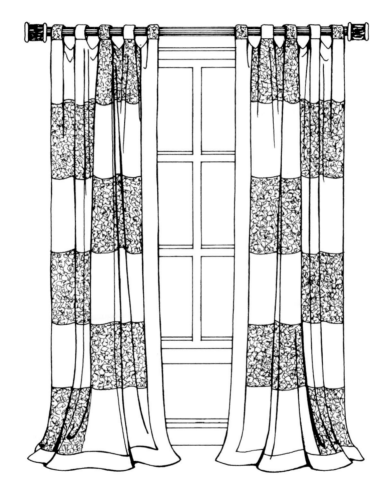

Image 164

Color blocked tab top panels with white banding fit through a three-inch
wood rod and puddle onto the floor. Great modern appeal!

Image 165
Butterfly pleated, color blocked panels glide easily back and forth on modern ring
and rod hardware.

Image 166

Triple blouson tops on the drapery panels draw the eye with their unique beauty.

Draperies

Image 167
Grommet topped drapery panels held back with coordinating fabric
tiebacks are simply modern.

Image 168

Cuffed panel valances over drapery panels provide an unusual look. The longer far edges of the valance pull the eye down and allow it to focus on the puddled fabric and trims on the floor.

Draperies

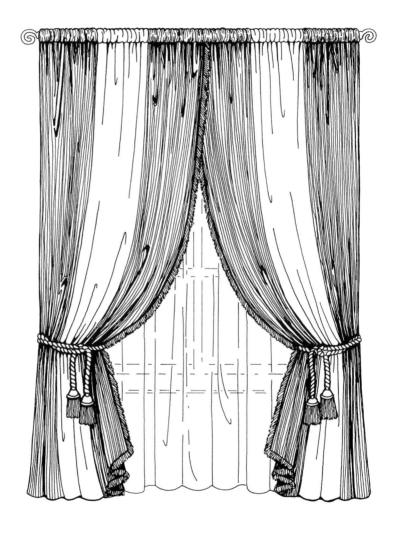

Image 169
Color blocked rod pocket drapery panels with sheer underdraperies
are lush and eye-catching.

Image 170
Unique knotted tab top drapery panels are fetching with coordinating tiebacks.

Draperies

Image 171
A padded, upholstered cornice with unique detailing is the perfect foil for double
drapery panels.

Image 172

Vertically striped drapery panels coordinate well with a matching, upholstered cornice and horizontally-striped fabric tiebacks crafted from the same fabric.

Draperies

Image 173

This scrumptious treatment mirrors fabric at the top on the Savannah shaped upholstered cornice and at the deep bottom hem.

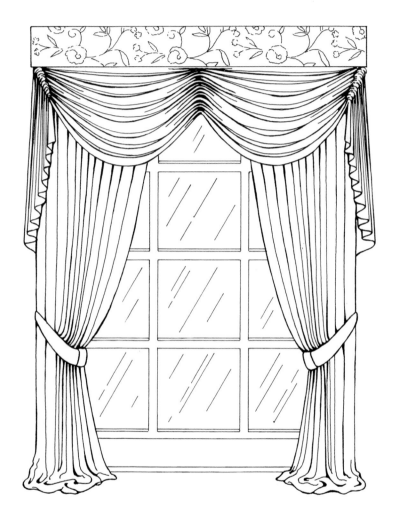

Image 174
An upholstered cornice holds a nine-pleated swag and cascade top treatment and
puddled drapery panels.

Draperies

Image 175
Crisply pleated drapery panels are contained by a scalloped soft cornice.

Image 176
A classic soft Savannah valance creates a comfortable country-style
window treatment.

Draperies

Image 177
A classic pole swag is offset by pleated drapery panels and flip top
bellpull-style ornaments.

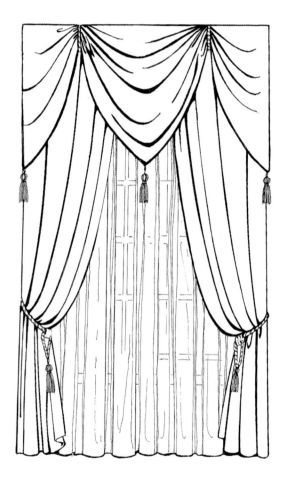

Image 178
A triangle handkerchief valance with tassel accent is the top layer in this three
layer treatment with sheer underdraperies and full side panels.

Draperies

Image 179
A handkerchief soft valance creates visual interest at the top of the window.
Drapery panels with matching fabric tiebacks on either side add softness.

Image 180
A soft triangle cornice is a dainty accent to the larger and more powerful pleated
and puddled drapery panels.

Draperies

Image 181
An offset triangle valance placed under a wood cornice but over a soft cornice
is an unusual twist. Pleated stationary drapery panels complete this
interesting treatment.

Image 182
Triple triangles placed over a soft cornice pull the eye up with the contrast fabric.
Note that the drapery panels have matching contrast fabric tiebacks.

Draperies

Image 183
Three shirred swags are peeking out from under a soft cornice. Double fabric
drapery panels tie the whole look together.

Flip top triangle valances with oversized tassels balance this otherwise
asymmetrical drapery panel treatment.

Draperies

Image 185

Opposites attract when dark and light fabrics combine into a powerful treatment.
A horizontally striped upholstered cornice is the perfect topper.

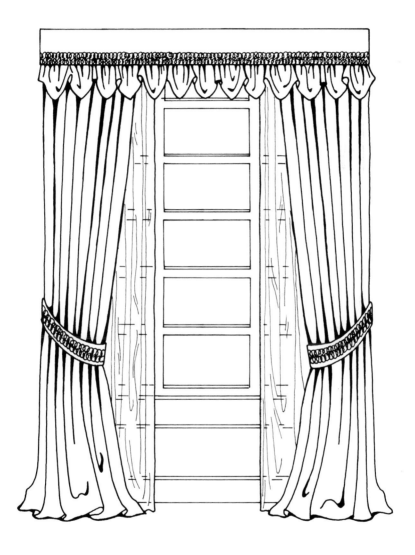

Image 186
A small bloused top treatment, sheer draperies and pleated panels with tiebacks to match the valance are clever together.

Draperies

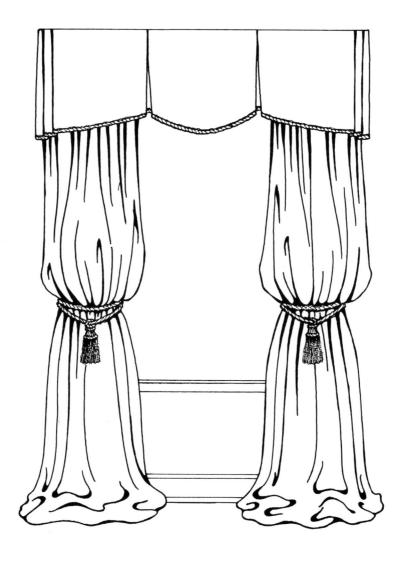

Image 187
A box pleated valance caps Bishop sleeve panels accented with tassels.

Image 188

An arched box pleated valance edged with brush fringe, paired with pleated, matching drapery panels are simply elegant.

Image 189
Color blocked drapery panels with button accents complements the cheerful
inverted box pleat valance.

Image 190
Bishop sleeve draperies with thickly braided ties and arched cornice follow the
window shape well without masking it.

Draperies

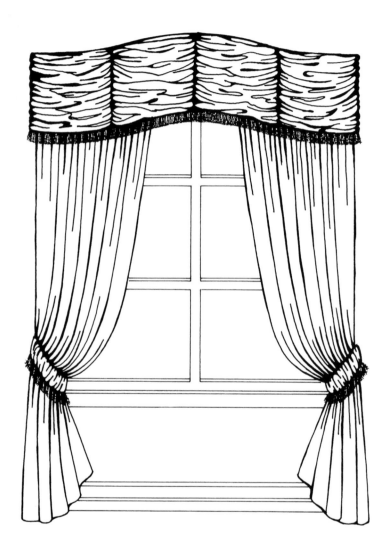

Image 191

An arched Austrian valance with brush fringe and stationary drapery panels with matching tiebacks could be just right in a master bedroom.

Image 192

Reminiscent of a flowing dancing dress, this scarf swag treatment accents the window without overpowering it.

Draperies

Image 193

Bay windows can be tricky to treat. This pleated panel and valance is a nice way to decorate a complicated window, simply.

Charles Randall's Designer Sketchfile

Image 194

Instead of hiding the shape of this grand window, a drapery treatment was chosen
to accent its graceful arch. Tassel detailing is an inspired choice.

Image 195

Stationary cuffed drapery panels soften the window frame, while the striped
Roman shade provides the privacy and sun control.

Image 196
Intriguing drapery hardware provides the focal point for this arch top window;
drapeable fabric provides the soft accent.

Draperies

Image 197
A large arched upholstered cornice with matching trillian cornices
showcase this enormous window as well as hold small swags and stately
Bishop sleeve drapery panels.

Image 198
Trillian cornices at top and bottom flank the doorway and hold the single swags at
the top—and the shirred vertical fabric treatments, too.

Draperies

Image 199
For this large picture window, upholstered trillian cornices accentuate the view;
swagged fabric in between and vertically softens, but does not impede, the view.

Swags & Cascades

Swags & Cascades

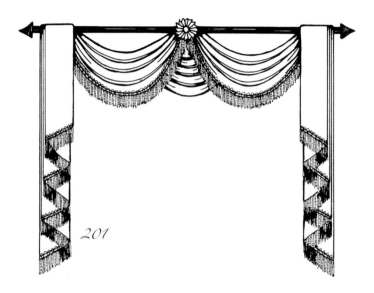

201

202

Image 201 & 202
(201) Stacked cascades over pleated swags, pole mounted with brush fringe and
rosette; (202) Classic gathered swags and cascades—board mounted

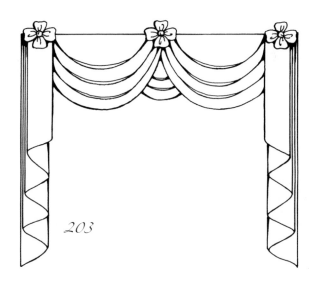

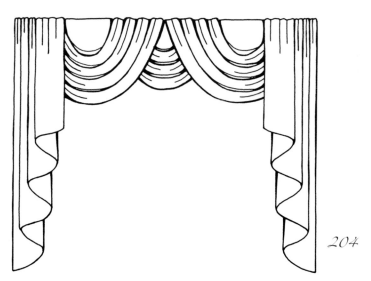

Image 203 & 204
(203) A classic board-mounted swag and cascade treatment with fabric flower accents; (204) Simple board-mounted swag and cascade lets beautiful fabric do the talking.

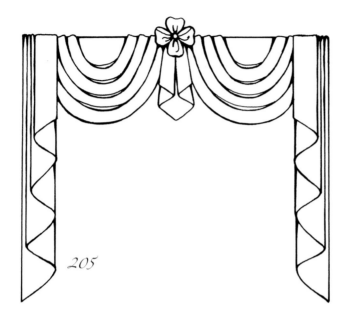

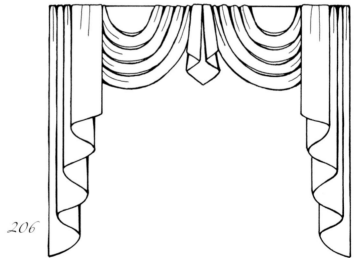

Image 205 & 206

(205) A board-mounted swag and cascade top treatment with jabot and fabric flower accent; (206) A simple board-mounted swag, cascade and jabot treatment.

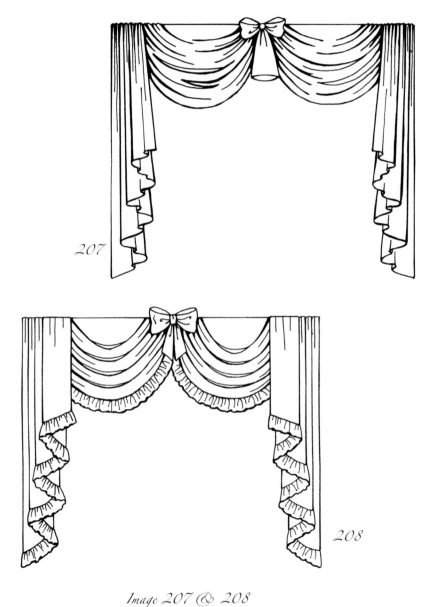

Image 207 & 208

(207) Deep pleats in this drapeable fabric make this swag and cascade treatment utterly feminine; (208) This swag and cascade treatment takes on a country feel with the ruffle trim and bow accent.

Swags & Cascades

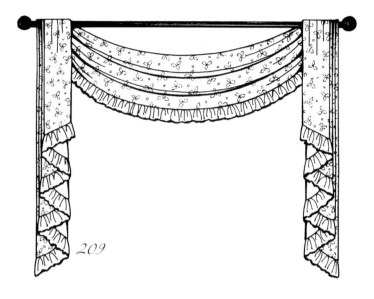

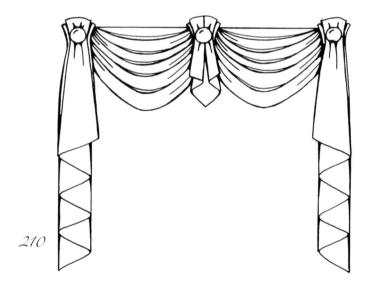

Image 209 & 210
(209) A simple pole swag and cascade top treatment with
ruffle trim; (210) Tailored swag and cascade elegance with large fabric-covered
button detailing.

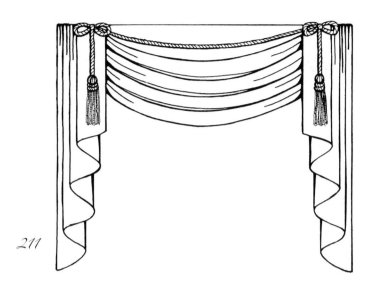

211

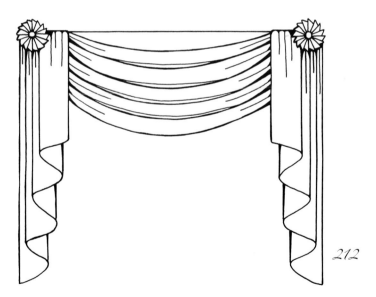

212

Image 211 & 212

(211) A board-mounted swag and cascade top treatment with tassel and braid detailing; (212) Board-mounted swag with flanking soft cascades and rosette accent on upper corners.

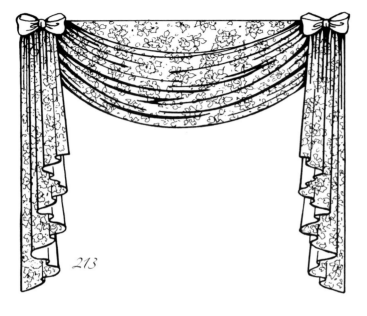

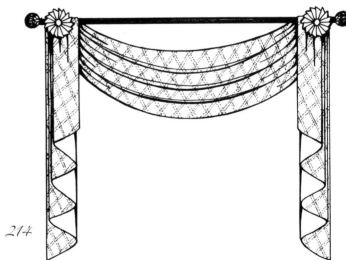

Image 213 & 214
(213) Board-mounted swag and cascade with contrast underlining and bow accents; (214) Pole mounted swag and cascades with contrast underlining and rosette accents.

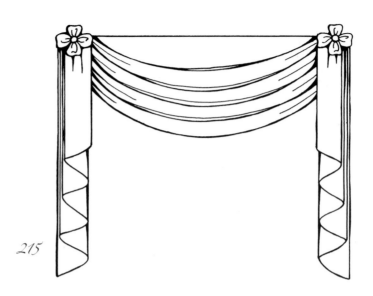

Image 215 & 216

(215) Board-mounted swag and jabot with rosette accent at each upper corner;
(216) Pole swag and jabot with contrast underlining and center rosette accent.

Fabric Shades

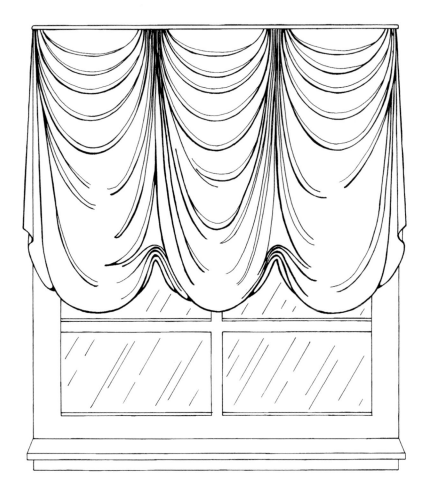

Image 301
Invisibly mounted cloud shade

Fabric Shades

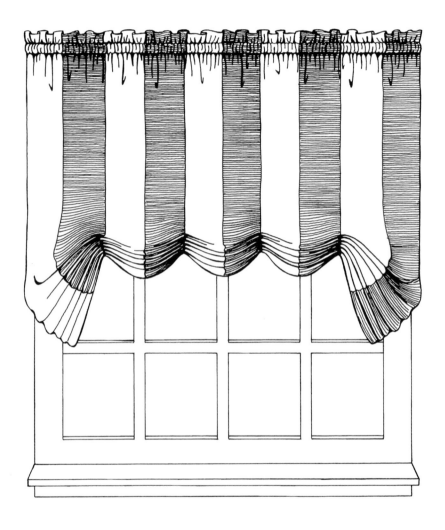

Image 302
Rod pocket soft specialty shade.

Image 303
Uniquely shaped turban swag cornice atop a classic balloon shade.

Fabric Shades

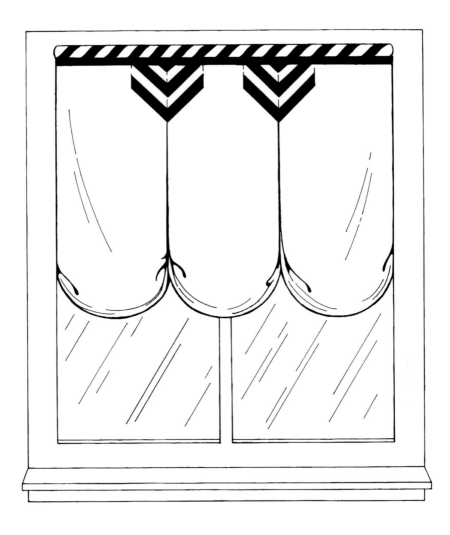

Image 304
Triangle accents draw the eye toward this balloon shade.

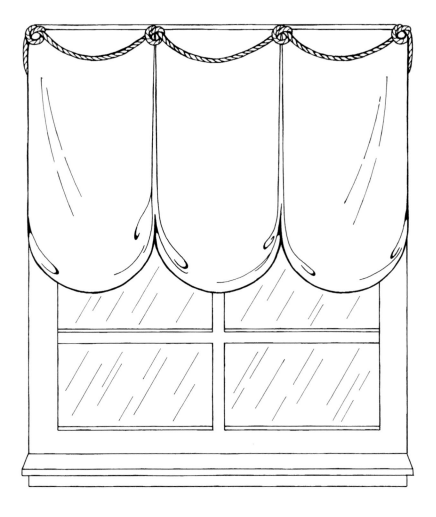

Image 305
Pleated balloon shade with braid trim accent.

Fabric Shades

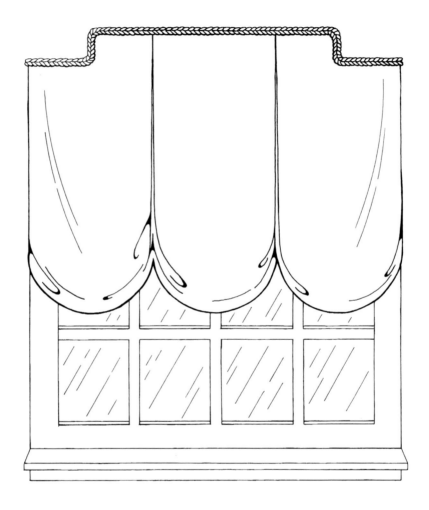

Image 306
Cut out corners on this balloon shade are a unique draw for the eye.

Image 307
A wood cornice with wallpaper insert offers seamless installation for the shirred
cloud shade.

Fabric Shades

Image 308
An overlapping triangle valance is a fine accompaniment to a patterned
Roman shade.

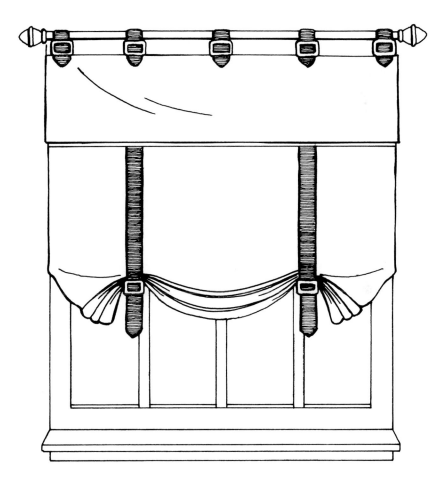

Image 309
Flat Roman shade held in place with leather straps. Note, too, the unique
buckle top tabs.

Fabric Shades

Image 310
Stagecoach shade with contrast straps.

Charles Randall's Designer Sketchfile

Image 311
A shirred cloud shade exhibits a matching blouson valance.

Fabric Shades

Image 312

This cloud shade achieves a full but tailored look by gathering fabric onto a horizontal rod. A short mock shade finishes the top nicely.

Image 313
Scalloped gathered valance with ruffles over a flat Roman shade with visible
drawing mechanism.

Fabric Shades

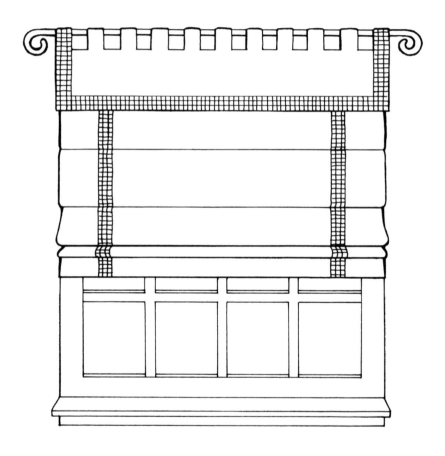

Image 314
With a unique tab top and contrast trim, this Roman shade delights.

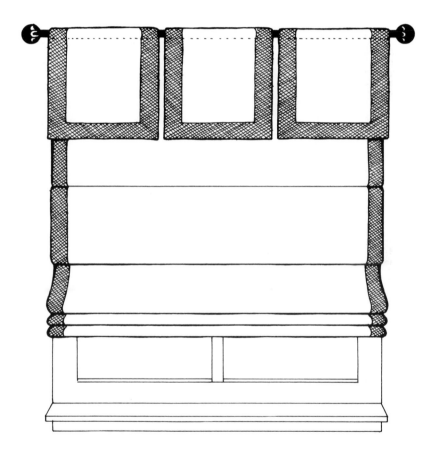

Image 315
A flat, simple Roman shade draws up into graceful folds. Rod pocket flags
decorate the front for additional interest.

Fabric Shades

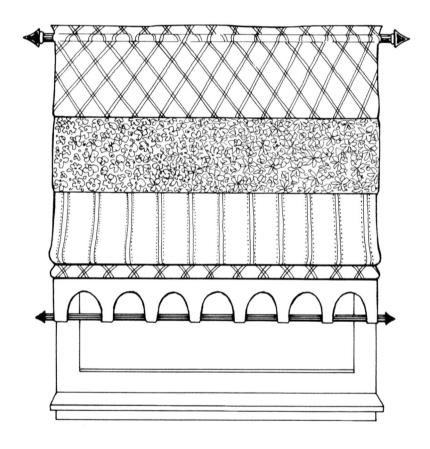

Image 316
Using multiple fabrics is creative and inspiring. Note, too, the mirror effect of the rod pocket top with the inverted tab and rod bottom.

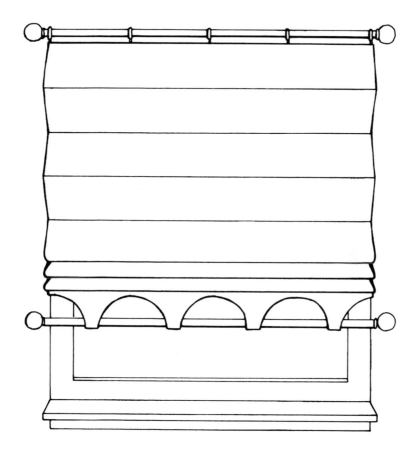

Image 317
Rod and rod top Roman shade with inverted tab and rod bottom.

Fabric Shades

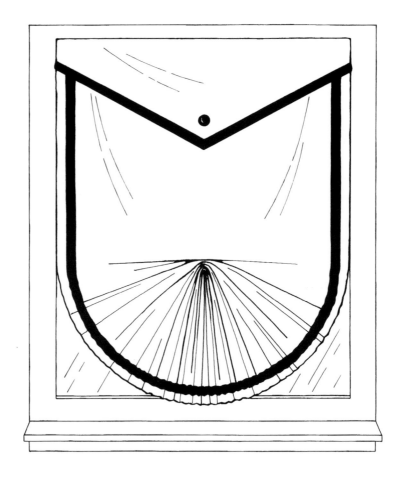

Image 318
Specialty fan shade with triangle valance top.

Image 319
The popular Roman shade made unusual through the color blocking of
every other pleat.

Image 320
Soft swag-style shade with shirred fabric-covered rod.

Image 321
Roman shade with contrast stripes and inverted pleat valance decorated with bows.

Fabric Shades

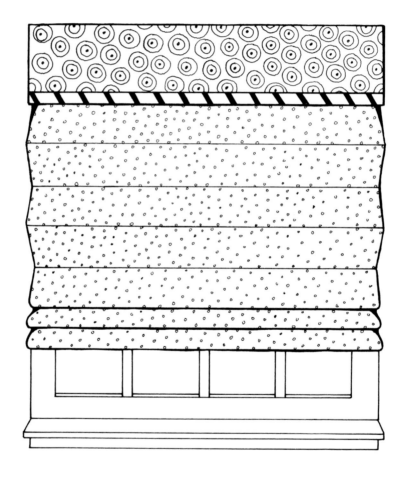

Image 322
Cheerful fabric combinations transform a Roman shade into the perfect window
treatment for any childs' room.

Bedding

Bedding

Image 401
Box pleated rectangles in both the bed valance and dust ruffle are tailored and elegant. Undulating tassel ties soften the mood.

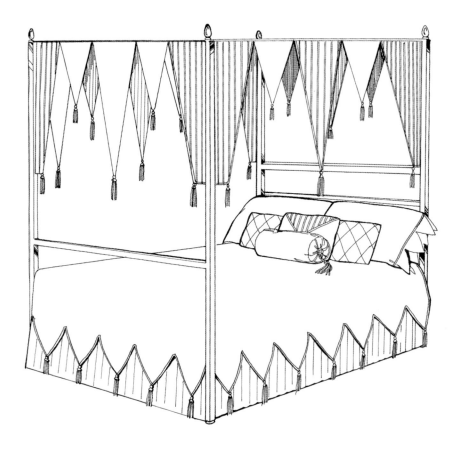

Image 402
Triangle valance flags with tassel accents are mirrored in the matching coverlet
and pillow cases.

Bedding

Image 403
Drapery panels, which can be closed for privacy, flank each side of the bed.
A soft cornice hangs from the detailed wood canopy, which matches the coverlet.

Image 404

A soft scalloped cornice with brush fringe is mirrored in both the luxe drapery panels and the box pleated bed skirt. Note, too, that the fabric is also used in the bolsters.

Bedding

Image 405

Elaborate bed posts could be a focal point but the entire bed ensemble shines with swagged fabric cascades at the back of the bed and unusual scalloped valance surrounding three sides. Matching brush fringe on the bedspread ties it all together.

Image 406
Box pleated, curved valance with shirred fabric ceiling; scalloped coverlet with
box pleated duster.

Bedding

Image 407
Upholstered headboard matches the gathered bed skirt, swags, jabots and drapery panels; luscious swags cap the top.

Image 408
Pencil pleated top treatment with matching side panels and bed skirt trimmed in
tassel fringe; upholstered headboard.

Bedding

Image 409

Unusual fabric scarves start at center, cascading down each of the four sides of the bed; scalloped coverlet with brush fringe; gathered bedskirt. matching upholstered headboard and pillows.

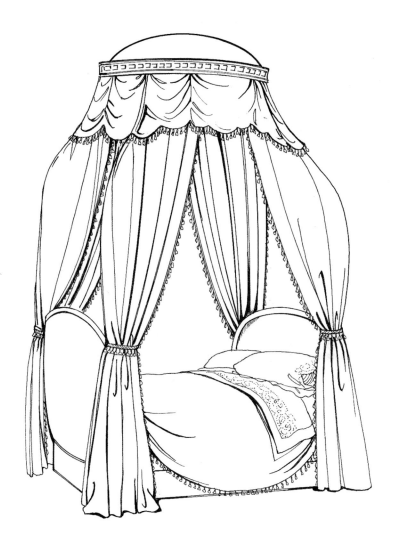

Image 410
An oval corona fit for a Queen with lush drapery panels and tassel and
fringe-imbued coverlet.

Bedding

Image 411
Crown corona with double Bishop sleeve panels, oversized tassel accents and
matching coverlet.

Image 412

Crown corona with cascade and bow accents, ruched upholstered headboard and
scalloped gathered bedskirt.

Bedding

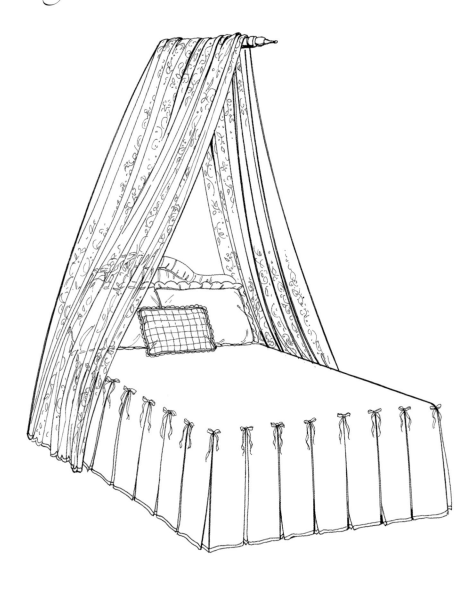

Image 413
Fabric draped over a decorative pole; box pleated coverlet with tassel accenting.

Image 414

Fabric draped over a decorative pole and secured with large tassel tiebacks;
scalloped dust ruffle with bolster pillows on the bed.

Bedding

Image 415
Pleated bedskirt with swag and rosette accent; fabric draped headboard with
bow accents.

Image 416
Scarf swags with small knotted cascade; matching upholstered headboard and
pleated bedskirt.

Bedding

Image 417
Box pleated bedskirt with braid-trimmed coverlet; floral drapery panels with
matching tiebacks and imposing goblet pleated top treatment with back curtain.
Matching pillows.

Image 418
A wood cornice holds pleated fabric valance and drapery panels; matching dust
ruffle; scalloped coverlet.

Bedding

Image 419
Horizontally arched Kingston valance with draperies and tassel tiebacks;
pleated dust ruffle with pillows to match.

Image 420
A half round corona with swag and jabot defines the area. Note how decorative
poles extend from the wall on either side of the bed to hold the draperies in place.
Swagged coverlet over box pleated dust ruffle and coordinated bolster finish.

Bedding

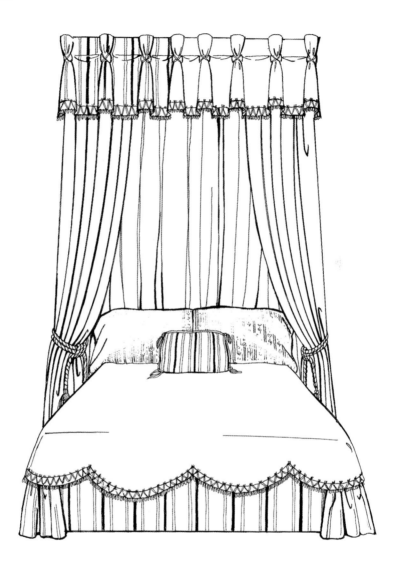

Image 421
Goblet pleated valance with unusually trimmed edge, lush draperies and matching
dust ruffle and pillow.

Image 422

Banner-style canopy is hung from decorative poles, suspended inches from
the ceiling with braided straps. Matching upholstered head and footboard with
scalloped brush fringe-trimmed dust ruffle.

Bedding

Image 423
Scalloped, box pleated valance is elegantly tailored. Pleated drapery panels with small scalloped edging. Deeply pleated bedskirt offers a feminine touch.

Image 424

Scarf swag hangs casually off two angled decorative rods. A slouchy comforter completes the look. Note, too, how the headboard mirrors the positioning of the rods.

Bedding

Image 425
Goblet pleated draperies are attached via rings off decorative rods, which
extend horizontally from the wall. Inverted box pleated dust ruffle with double
braid and tassels.

Image 426

Ruched fabric is seen on the headboard, corona and bed's lower edge. Pleated drapery panels held in place with decorative hardware and matching coverlet complete this ensemble.

Bedding

Image 427
Lush Bishop sleeve panels are set off by an elaborately swagged cornice; matching
pleated dust ruffle and coordinating pillows.

Image 428

A boxy cornice with shell motif holds a pretty swag and cascade top treatment as well as full, pleated drapery panels with braided tassel tiebacks. Coordinated coverlet; upholstered headboard.

Bedding

Image 429
An elaborately gathered circular corona with elaborate trimming; drapery panels
with contrast lining and dust ruffle in a coordinating fabric.

Image 430

Swag draped corona with lushly edged pleated draperies contained by decorative rosettes; pleated dust ruffle; matching coverlet (note how the same trim has been echoed on the coverlet in a unique way).

Bedding

Image 431
Soft cornice lined in welt houses wide drapery panels; simple box pleated
comforter touts the same welt. Ruched scalloped headboard.

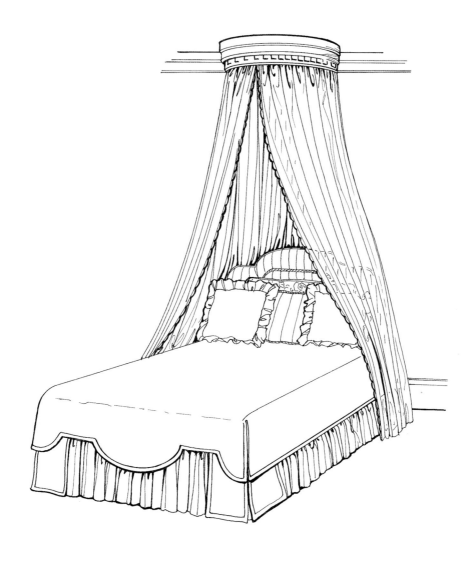

Image 432
Simple circular corona holds sheer fabric panels. Upholstered headboard, scalloped
coverlet and box pleated dust ruffle enhance.

Bedding

Image 433

Goblet pleated valance with a slight curve, jabot and braided tassel accents and inverted box pleat dust ruffle with coordinating pillows.

Image 434

Gathered valance showcases an elaborate fabric bed ceiling with matching dust skirt and draperies.

Bedding

Image 435

The traditional canopy apparatus is unnecessary in this installation, where fabric is applied directly to the ceiling and then swagged slightly to create architectural interest. Matching dust ruffle, pillows and headboard. Decorative bows.

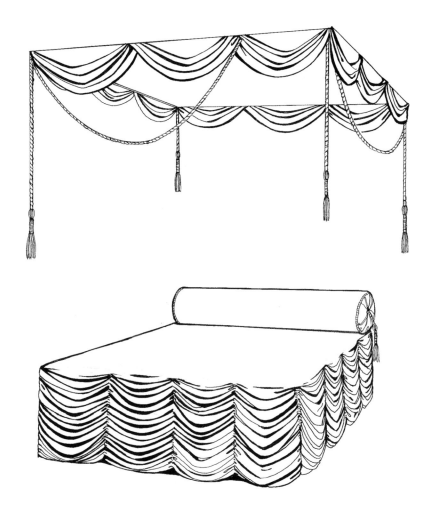

Image 436
Fabric is applied directly to the ceiling and then swagged on all four sides,
punctuated with braid and tassels. An elaborate Austrian-style coverlet is
quite dramatic.

Bedding

Image 437
Swags and jabots with tassel trim decorate both the top and bottom of this bed
ensemble; a box pleated valance and dust ruffle complete it.

Image 438

Criss-crossing lattice work passementerie on the canopy, overlapping triangles on the coverlet and a gathered dust ruffle make for a simply elegant ensemble.

Bedding

Image 439
Flouncy drapery panels edged in lace with matching bedskirt and pillows; note the
fabric ceiling: very feminine.

Image 440

This tailored bed ensemble displays box pleating with the horizontal lines of a soft
swag both top and bottom. Decorative tassels add a designer touch.

Bedding

Image 441

An arched canopy bed with thick tassel fringe is a little girls' delight. Matching coverlet and drapery panels are very pretty.

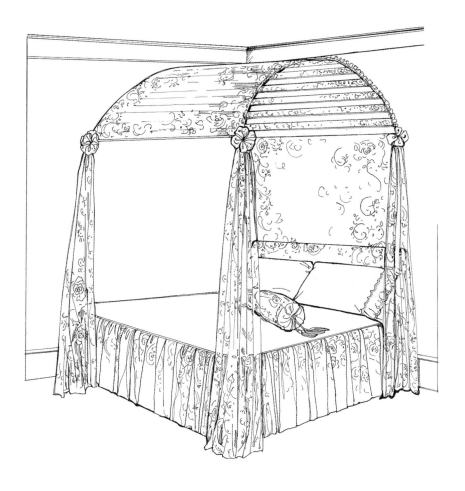

Image 442
Long pinch pleated dust ruffle with coordinating headboard, drapery panels
and topper.

Bedding

Image 443

This simple arrangement, especially perfect for a guest room, displays tent top-like canopy with matching dust ruffle, bedding and pillows.

Image 444
Crisp box pleating married with ruched fabric on the upper canopy, headboard
and bedspread are nicely tailored.

Bedding

Image 445
Deep drooping swags and jabots with contrast banding are a delightful foil when
used in conjunction with a simple coverlet and pleated dust ruffle.

Image 446

Cuffed draperies with a tab top are gathered smartly into an hourglass shape
with matching fabric tiebacks. Coordinating dust ruffle and pillow trim finish
this treatment.

Image 447

Elaborately trimmed fabric is installed just slightly above the bedposts and then wrapped organically. Coordinating pillows and bedding complete.

Image 448
A sheer scarf swag loops around the metal bed hardware in an almost
asymmetrical style. A sheer coverlet is a lovely accent.

Bedding Alcoves

Image 501

Making the most of this angled alcove, a scarf swag with large center jabot echoes the wall angles. A second swag with cascades hangs effortlessly across the window. Coordinating bedskirt and fabric covered box at the footer complete.

Bedding Alcoves

Image 502

Tab top wide draperies hung on a decorative rod, shower curtain-style, can cover the sleeping area completely when released from the tieback. Note, too, that the headboard has tab detailing.

Image 503
A small architectural inset is made wonderfully useful by adding a soft, embellished
cornice with coordinating bed coverlet. Note that a fabric bed panel was inserted
between the bed and the wall. Draperies, for privacy, are a finishing touch.

Bedding Alcoves

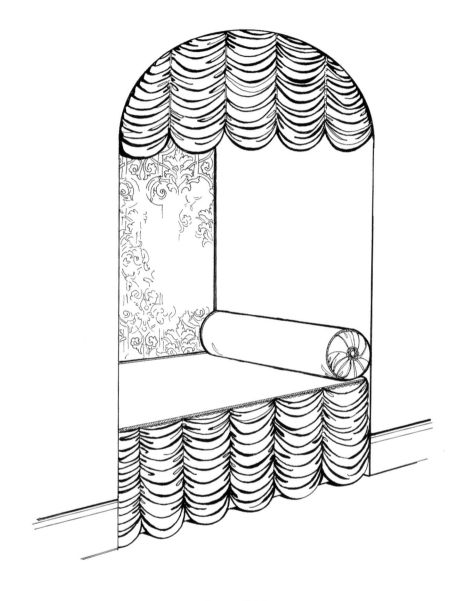

Image 504
An Austrian valance and coordinating bedskirt.

Image 505
Pretty drapery accent panels make this alcove all the more cozy.
Scalloped coverlet adds interest and flair.

Bedding Alcoves

Image 506

Tie tab drapery panels can easily be released from their tiebacks to
provide complete privacy. Note that the headboard has tie tab pillows attached
as an accent.

Image 507

Pleated valance and bedskirt with upholstered headboard and drapery panel make
great use of this tucked in space.

Bedding Alcoves

Image 508
Romantic country florals with ruffle accent cover this small area beautifully.

Image 509

Smart swags with rosette accents at the top and bottom; Bishop sleeve panels and
upholstered sideboard.

Bedding Alcoves

Image 510
A tiny daybed area with upholstered walls and ceiling; pleated panels and soft cornice with jabot accents.

Image 511

Arched goblet pleated valance with matching draperies accents this tiny sleigh bed;
pleated coverlet with coordinating pillows; tassel tiebacks with
decorative hardware.

Bedding Alcoves

Image 512
Drapery panels are hung into the sloped ceiling and held back with casual fabric
bows. Headboard and pillows have matching fabric. Contrast comforter.

Drapery Headers

Drapery Headers

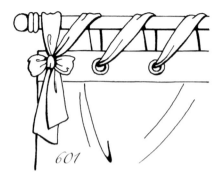

601

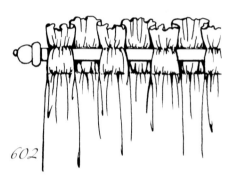

602

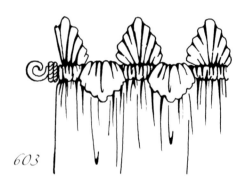

603

Images 601, 602 & 603
(601) Grommet and tie top; (602) Unique ruched tab top;
(603) Shell motif with fabric covered rod and mock tab top

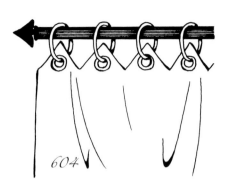

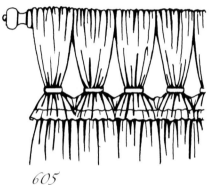

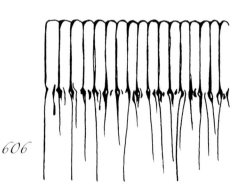

Images 604, 605 & 606
(604) Grommet top with rings; (605) Butterfly pleated tab top;
(606) Pencil pleated rod pocket top

Drapery Headers

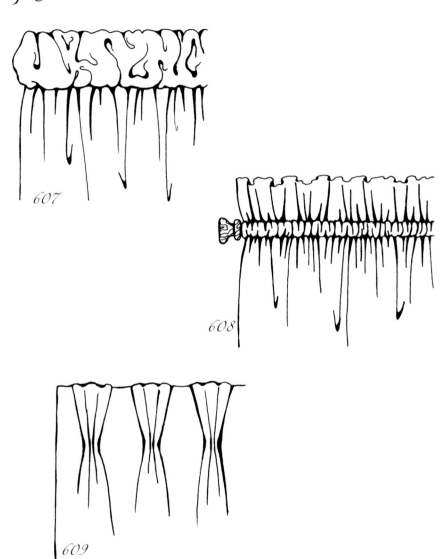

Images 607, 608 & 609
(607) Blouson header with gathered pleats; (608) Rod pocket header with ruffle
accent top; (609) Butterfly pleated drapery hung from sewn in hooks

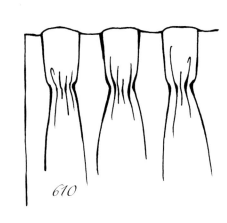

610

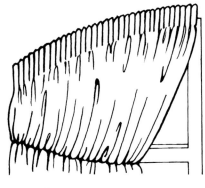

611

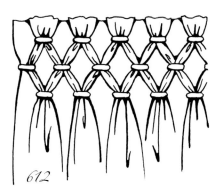

612

Images 610, 611 & 612

(610) Slightly gathered cartridge pleated drapery header hung from sewn in hooks;
(611) Pencil pleated arch top drapery; (612) Designer header with unusual
lattice work detailing

Drapery Headers

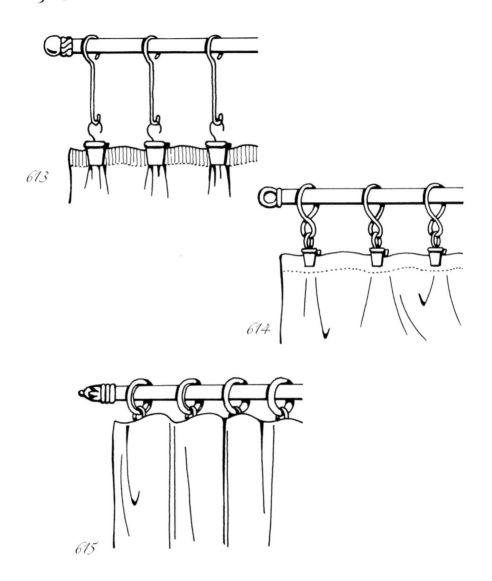

Images 613, 614 & 615

(613) Unusual rod and ring header with fan pleated drapery; (614) Clip on drapery
hardware in use with a flat panel drapery; (615) Traditional rod and ring header
with stitched in rings

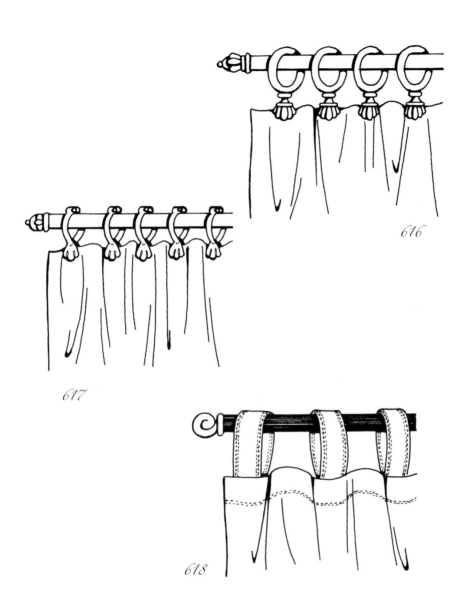

Images 616, 617 & 618
(616) Designer rod and ring header for flat panel draperies; (617) Shower curtain
style rod and rings; (618) Gathered tab top drapery header

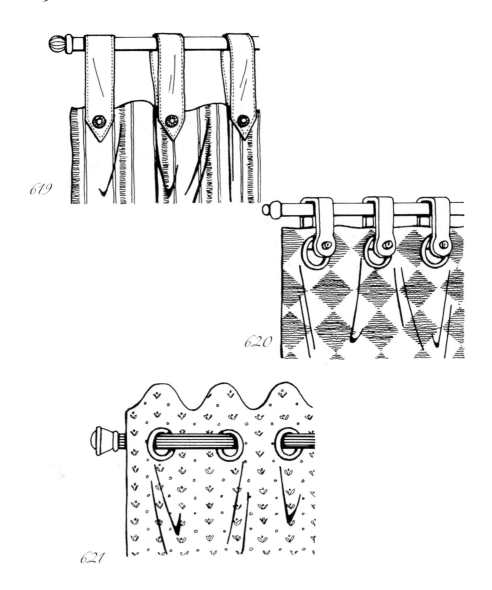

Images 619, 620 & 621

(619) Button tab top drapery on decorative rod; (620) Grommet top header on flat panel drapery with unusual rectangular-shaped rings; (621) In-and-out grommet drapery header with scalloped top on slightly gathered flat panel

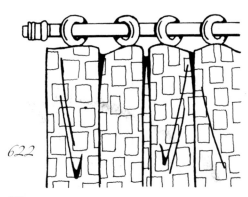

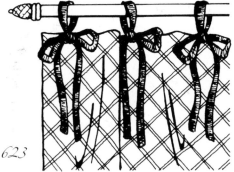

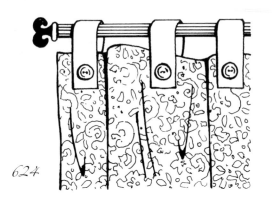

Images 622, 623 & 624

(622) Cuffed drapery panel with ring and rod hardware; (623) Tie tab top drapery
header; (624) Button flap drapery header over decorative rod

About the CD ROM

On the enclosed disc you will find two folders. The first, entitled LR, contains a series of folders for each of this book's chapters, labeled accordingly. Inside are low resolution images—everything you see in the book, you will find in these folders as well. For the record, low resolution images are typically used on websites or "for position only" in printed documents because they take up very little "space" or megabytes.

The second folder, labeled PDF, houses the same images as the LR folder, only they are in a portable data file format, created from high resolution images.

We took the time to have the images our talented artists drew scanned slowly and in as high a resolution as possible, so you will even find that these images are clear and concise. This is our way of bringing you the best possible quality images for you—and your clients.

Open the images. Print them out if you like—and get out a set of watercolors, colored pencils or even crayons. Try out different colors on your images. Print them on transparent paper and layer images over each other. This is the way you can create your own individual and very unique window treatment for your next exciting project.

It is this experimentation with color, pattern and shape that makes our projects truly exciting and exclusive. I hope you will be quite inspired.